BBC CHILDREN'S BOOKS
Published by the Penguin Group
Penguin Books Ltd, 80 Strand, London, WC2R 0RL, England
Penguin Group (USA) Inc., 375 Hudson Street, New York, New York 10014, USA
Penguin Books (Australia) Ltd, 250 Camberwell Road, Camberwell, Victoria 3124, Australia.
(A division of Pearson Australia Group Pty Ltd)
Canada, India, New Zealand, South Africa
Published by BBC Children's Books, 2006
Text and design © Children's Character Books, 2006
Written by Stephen Cole
6
ISBN-13: 978-1-40590-231-1
ISBN-10: 1-40590-231-0
Printed in Great Britain by Clays Ltd, St Ives plc

DOCTOR · WHO

QUIZ BOOK 2

CONTENTS

THE POWER, THE PASSION, THE PINSTRIPES!

The Doctor's changed his face before and he may well do it again. But do YOU have what it takes to fill the Tenth Doctor's sneakers? Take this test to see if you could truly be the TARDIS's next tenant!

1. **An alien warlord challenges you to a contest of strength — but if you lose, planet Earth is doomed. Do you:**

a) Implore the warlord that violence is not the answer. There has to be another way to settle your differences.

b) Take him on fair and square, trusting that your Time Lord powers and sheer gall will see you through.

c) Distract him and strike him down from behind — it might not be very fair, but there's a planet at stake!

2. You are summoned by a mysterious, enigmatic creature who wishes to meet you but won't say why. Do you:

a) Send a message back saying you'll meet, but only on neutral turf once you've checked it's safe. You don't want to risk Rose's life.

b) Drop everything and go at once. You love chucking yourself into a new mystery.

c) Decide not to go, that's got to be a trap!

3. Finding yourself to be in Scotland, you run into a starchy old monarch. Do you:

a) Observe her from a respectful distance. If you involve her in one of your adventures you risk changing history.

b) Knock about with her and see what she's like. When will you get another opportunity like this?

c) Excuse yourself and get back to the real work of finding evil monsters to fight.

4. When UFOs are spotted over a school and the pupils start getting top grades, what do you do?

a) Start scanning local space for UFO fuel signatures. Those will help you identify the alien visitors and see if they're a threat.

b) Impersonate a supply teacher and try to find out more first-hand.

c) Set traps for any possible aliens around the school, and see what you snag.

5. The TARDIS lands on a weird planet that reason insists should not exist. Do you:

a) Take careful measurements to check the systems aren't on the blink, then formulate theories as to how the planet can possibly be there.

b) Have a look around and check it out — you never want to listen to reason.

c) Take off immediately and head for a pleasure planet instead.

6. **You and Rose fancy watching an old rock and roll gig in the 1970s. Do you:**

a) Spend a couple of hours charting a careful course. You don't want to miss this!

b) Whack on a loud CD of the band to get you in the mood and get hitting those switches!

c) Set the TARDIS to take you backstage so you can watch the band from the wings.

7. **What do you consider your greatest weapon against evil?**

a) Your sonic screwdriver.

b) Your gob.

c) Your fists.

8. **The Cybermen and Daleks are both invading the Earth at once. Do you:**

a) Duck into the TARDIS library and look up some of the strategies employed in the Time War to pick up fighting tips.

b) Try to set one side against the other to buy you time for inspiration to strike.

c) Blow up everyone and everything. Earth was finished in any case.

Mostly As:

You're perhaps a bit too thoughtful
and considered for ramshackle
adventures through time and space. All
the planning in the cosmos can't make
you prepared for some of the horrors
you will face, and in dangerous situations,
a spoonful of spontaneity can mean the difference between life and death. So
while your answers aren't necessarily wrong, try and loosen up and enjoy your
travels too. Only by plunging headlong into the Doctor's life can you hope to get
the most out of it.

Mostly Bs:

You think very like the Tenth Doctor, with an instinctive desire to lose yourself in
mayhem then blag your way out of it with off-the-cuff plans, fast-talking and even
faster thinking. But while it's cool you're so attuned to the Doctor's way of living,
it's important you bring some of your own personality to the job as well.

Mostly Cs:

Blimey! With you in the TARDIS, who knows what would happen! You're too much
in a rush to fully enjoy madcap adventures in time and space. Chill a little. Part
of the fun is leaving yourself open to the *possibilities* of time-space travel, even
the unlikeliest character in the most improbable location could lead you to the
most amazing adventure of your life. While your selfish streak dominates your
actions, you'll never know — so loosen up!

THE CHRISTMAS INVASION
TRUE OR FALSE?

One Christmas, the Earth was nearly invaded by the terrifying Sycorax... but were you scoffing too much festive grub to notice? Say whether the statements below are true or false.

1. **The Sycorax craft swallowed a space probe heading for Venus.**
   TRUE/FALSE

2. **They used the blood sample on board the probe to control all humans with that blood group.**
   TRUE/FALSE

3. **They wanted to give the human race to other aliens as Christmas presents.**
   TRUE/FALSE

4. **The Doctor was recovering from his regeneration and was very weak.**
   TRUE/FALSE

5. **The American President was transported to the Sycorax ship.**
   TRUE/FALSE

6. **With the Doctor out of action, Rose tried to stop the Sycorax single-handed.**
   TRUE/FALSE

7. **It went really well.**
   TRUE/FALSE

8. **The Doctor recovered and broke the Sycorax's control of humanity.**
   TRUE/FALSE

9. **He finally defeated the Sycorax leader with a satsuma.**
   TRUE/FALSE

10. **The Prime Minister had the Sycorax ship destroyed.**
    TRUE/FALSE

A NEW DOCTOR

Just as we thought we were getting to know the Doctor, he changed into another person! How much do you know about the new model? Put your knowledge to the test...

1. **Which of the following best describes the Doctor's suit?**

a) Brown.

b) Baggy.

c) Brown with pinstripes.

2. **What does the Doctor sometimes wear to help his eyesight?**

a) Chunky-frame glasses.

b) A monocle.

c) Contact lenses.

3. What does the Doctor wear on his feet?

a) Sneakers.

b) Riding boots.

c) Flip-flops.

4. What was he wearing when he first arrived on Earth after regenerating?

a) A dressing gown.

b) A leather jacket.

c) A toga.

5. What came out of the Doctor's mouth as his regeneration started to settle down?

a) Wisps of golden energy.

b) A sandwich.

c) A distress signal.

6. How many hearts does he have now he's regenerated?

a) One.

b) Two.

c) Three.

7. **What finally made the Doctor wake up from his post-regeneration coma?**

a) A headache pill.

b) The smell of soup.

c) The smell of tea.

8. **During his first adventure, what part of the Doctor's body was sliced off by the Sycorax leader?**

a) His foot.

b) His hand.

c) His knee.

9. **What did the Doctor say was weird just after regenerating?**

a) Having new teeth.

b) Having new arms.

c) Having visitors come to tea.

10. How many chances will the Doctor give menacing aliens?

a) Only one — he's that kind of man.

b) Two — he likes to be reasonable.

c) Three — third time lucky.

NEW EARTH TRUE OR FALSE?

The Doctor takes Rose further into the future than she's ever been before – beyond the year five billion! Do you remember their terrifying adventure on New Earth? If so, say whether the statements below are true or false.

1. **The Doctor was summoned to New Earth by the Face of Boe.**
   TRUE/FALSE

2. **He and Rose met nurses that looked like dogs.**
   TRUE/FALSE

3. **The wicked Cassandra was hiding in the hospital.**
   TRUE/FALSE

4. **She put her mind into Rose's body.**
   TRUE/FALSE

5. **Cassandra wanted to become a nurse at the hospital.**
   TRUE/FALSE

6. The nurses used natural herbal treatments on their patients.
TRUE/FALSE

7. The hospital was overrun by zombies infected with every illness in the universe.
TRUE/FALSE

8. Cassandra was unable to put her mind into the Doctor's body.
TRUE/FALSE

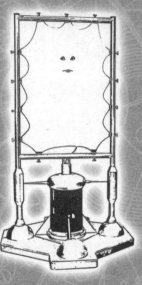

9. The Doctor healed all the zombies with a colourful cocktail of cures.
TRUE/FALSE

10. Cassandra escaped New Earth in a space shuttle.
TRUE/FALSE

SCORES:

8–10 Do you actually live in New New York? You are an expert on New Earth!

5–7 Not bad, but don't let the applegrass grow under your feet!

0–4 Is there something wrong with your brain? Don't worry — the Sisters can cure you…

ANSWERS:

1. True. 2. False. 3. True. 4. True. 5. False.

6. False. 7. True. 8. False. 9. True. 10. False.

SPACESHIP STUFF

1. **What was the name of the British space probe captured by the Sycorax?**

a) Guinevere One.

b) Lancelot Three.

c) Gulliver Two.

2. **What caused the systems failure on board the SS *Madame de Pompadour*?**

a) Collision with a meteor.

b) Attack from an alien craft.

c) An ion storm.

3. **What does a Sycorax spaceship most resemble out of the following:**

a) A giant rock.

b) A huge forest.

c) A roaring ocean.

4. How can you reach the planet Krop Tor?

a) In a rocket ship, travelling through a gravity funnel.

b) By teleport.

c) By space-walking from a star-station.

5. What objects filled the skies over the parallel Earth?

a) Aeroplanes.

b) Space shuttles.

c) Zeppelins.

6. What is a Void Ship?

a) A vessel that blows itself up after one journey.

b) A vessel designed to exist outside space and time.

c) A ship designed to avoid all other ships in busy space lanes.

7. How old was the SS _Madame de Pompadour_?

a) 37 years.

b) A million years.

c) 3,000 years.

8. How did the Doctor stop Zachary Blane's rocket from falling into a black hole?

a) He boosted its engines.

b) He used the TARDIS to tow it to safety.

c) He reversed the linearity of the proton flow.

ODD ONE OUT

Look at the different groups of people, places and things below. In each case, which is the odd one out, and why?

1. Chip, Yvonne from Torchwood, Tobey Zed when possessed.

2. The 2012 Olympics, The 1978 FA Cup Final, the 1953 Coronation.

3. Mickey, Rose, Jackie, Mickey's gran.

4. The Isolus, the Beast, the Daleks, Cassandra on New Earth.

5. Queen Victoria, The President of Britain, King Louis XV.

6. The Cybermen, the clockwork droids, the Daleks, surveillance cameras on board SS *Madame de Pompadour*.

ANSWERS:

1. Yvonne — the others have strange patterns marked on their faces.

2. The 1978 FA Cup Final — the other events were happening while the Doctor and Rose were battling aliens.

3. Rose — the others had human counterparts in the parallel Earth.

4. The Daleks — the others were capable of 'possessing' human bodies.

5. The British President — the others all belong to a royal family.

6. The clockwork droids — they are purely mechanical, while the others combine organic parts with machinery.

SCORES:

5–6 Excellent! Your powers of reasoning are almost as sharp as the Doctor's!

3–4 Not bad — you can reason things up, but sometimes you give up too easily...

1–2 Oh dear. You should really think about things harder!

0 Which is the odd one out — loser, loser, loser, YOU? Oops! There *isn't* an odd one out!

CYBER-QUIZ

The Doctor has met the Cybermen before on his travels through time and space. But when the TARDIS falls through a crack in time into a parallel world, he finds an entirely new breed, deadlier than ever... How much do you know about the steel giants?

1. What was John Lumic's ultimate aim in creating the Cybermen?

a) To keep alive the human brain at all costs.

b) To create a race of robot waiters.

c) To perfect cyber-surgery techniques.

2. What do all Cybermen carry on their chest?

a) A gun.

b) The Cybus Industries logo.

c) An identity tag.

3. **What stops a Cyberman from feeling anything?**

a) A pain-restraint harness.

b) A solitude circuit.

c) An emotional inhibitor.

4. **What do Cybermen say when they are going to kill somebody?**

a) Exterminate!

b) Annihilate!

c) Delete!

5. **How do Cybermen 'upgrade' humans?**

a) They convert them into Cybermen.

b) They replace their brains with computers.

c) They infect them with a special metal virus.

6. **Who became the first Cyber Controller?**

a) Jackie Tyler.

b) The Emperor Dalek.

c) John Lumic.

7. **What did Mrs Moore use to destroy a Cyberman in the cyber-factory?**

a) A laser gun.

b) An electromagnetic bomb.

c) An amplified scream.

8. **How did the Doctor defeat the Cybermen on the parallel world?**

a) He made them aware of the reality of their butchered existence.

b) He shut down their power supply.

c) He flooded their base with water.

YOUR LIFE IN THEIR HANDS

Should you find yourself unwell on New Earth in the year five billion, it pays to choose your hospital with care — the most advanced medical facility may not be the safest...

1. **The hospital visited by the Doctor and Rose was run by which Sisters?**

a) The Sisters of Mercy.

b) The Sisters of Plenitude.

c) The Sisters of Felinity.

2. **Which animals did the Sisters resemble?**

a) Stoats.

b) Badgers.

c) Cats.

3. **What is the one thing the Sisters cannot cure?**

a) The common cold.

b) Old age.

c) Voltepp's nose virus.

4. **What important New Earth dignitary is being treated for Petrifold Regression?**

a) The Duke of Manhattan.

b) The Earl of New Jersey.

c) The Lord of Brooklyn.

5. **What does the Petrifold Regression do to you?**

a) It makes you regress to childhood.

b) It makes your body shrivel up.

c) It turns your whole body to stone.

6. **What was the name of the matron who led the sisters?**

a) Casp.

b) Clasp.

c) Bukkal.

7. **Which of the following diseases was *not* mentioned in the hospital?**

a) Marconi's Disease.

b) Palindrome Pancrosis.

c) Zalofar's Contagion.

8. **Where do the sisters develop their incredible cures?**

a) In test tubes.

b) In specially grown human flesh.

c) In an orbiting medi-capsule.

9. What happens to any 'patients' in the Intensive Care Unit that show signs of real life?

a)   They are set free.

b)   They are incinerated.

c)   They are disintegrated.

10. What name does the Doctor give the new sub-species of humanity that he has cured of the Sisters' diseases?

a)   Super-humans.

b)   New humans.

c)   Proto-humans.

SCORES:

8–10   Your brain checks out fit and well. You can leave the hospital any time you like!

5–7   Your brain may be a bit run down. Book yourself in for a mind massage!

0–4   Oh dear. Bio-cattle and done-meat know more than you do! Next time watch more closely… for a sinister Sister could be watching YOU!

ANSWERS:

1. b	2. c	3. b	4. a	5. c
6. a	7. c	8. b	9. b	10. b

30

BEWARE THE WOLF
TRUE OR FALSE?

If there's a full moon outside, be very careful while doing this quiz. If the pages start sprouting hairs, drop the book and run! In the meantime, say whether the statements below are true or false.

1. The Doctor and Rose met Queen Victoria in Scotland.
    TRUE/FALSE

2. Rose had never been to the 19th century before.
    TRUE/FALSE

3. They all stopped for the night at a house called Torchwood.
    TRUE/FALSE

4. Warrior monks tried to expose Queen Victoria to a werewolf creature.
    TRUE/FALSE

5. The werewolf was friendly and joined her for supper.
    TRUE/FALSE

6. **The werewolf had a fierce aversion to mistletoe.**
TRUE/FALSE

7. **It chased the Doctor, Rose and Queen Victoria into a broom cupboard.**
TRUE/FALSE

8. **The Doctor defeated the werewolf using a telescope and a big diamond to amplify a beam of moonlight.**
TRUE/FALSE

9. **Queen Victoria gave the Doctor and Rose medals for their services.**
TRUE/FALSE

10. **Queen Victoria founded the Torchwood Institute to help protect Britain from similar strange phenomena.**
TRUE/FALSE

SCORES:

8–10 You would fight tooth and claw to achieve the best score!

5–7 Not exactly a howling success but not a disaster either.

0–4 You must have been watching through the wrong end of the telescope to score this low!

ANSWERS:

1. True. 2. False. 3. True. 4. True. 5. False.
6. True. 7. False. 8. True. 9. False. 10. True.

BRING ON THE MONSTERS!

The Doctor and Rose are monster experts, but how do you compare? Stop shivering in the shadows and put your knowledge to the test!

1. **We all know what a werewolf is, but how would the Doctor describe it?**

a)   A hairy beastie with teeth and claws.

b)   A lupine-wavelength-haemovariform.

c)   A creature of moonlit darkness.

2. **Which of the following was a previous form of the bat-like Krillitanes?**

a) Humans with long necks.

b) Tortoises with big feet.

c) Cybermen with no arms.

3. **Which creatures have an artificially grown nervous system threaded through their armoured suits?**

a) Daleks.

b) Cassandra's spiders.

c) Cybermen.

4. **How did the evil Wire become a disembodied entity?**

a) It was executed by its own people.

b) A terrible accident split its mind from its body.

c) It was born that way.

5. **What parts of the Abzorbaloff's victims end up reappearing over his body?**

a) The eyes.

b) The face.

c) The bottom.

6. **How many Cybermen from the parallel universe invaded our world?**

a) Five hundred.

b) Five million.

c) Five billion.

7. **What colour are an Ood's eyes when possessed by the Beast?**

a) White.

b) Red.

c) Stripy white-and-pink.

8. **How do the Daleks refer to a battle against the Cybermen?**

a) The Cyber Apocalypse.

b) Pest control.

c) Skaro War Seven.

FRIENDS REUNITED
TRUE OR FALSE?

A sinister school was the last place the Doctor expected to run into old friends... But here is your homework — say whether the statements below are true or false.

1. The Doctor posed as a dinner lady to gain entrance to a suspiciously sinister school.
    TRUE/FALSE

2. Rose posed as a supply teacher.
    TRUE/FALSE

3. The Doctor ran into his old friend Sarah Jane Smith.
    TRUE/FALSE

4. Hideous, bat-like aliens called Krillitanes had taken over the school.
    TRUE/FALSE

5. Canteen chips cooked in Krillitanes oil were making the children super-smart.
    TRUE/FALSE

6. **The Krillitanes were using the children's minds to solve tricky long division sums.**
TRUE/FALSE

7. **A robot dog called K-9 helped the Doctor fight the Krillitanes.**
TRUE/FALSE

8. **As the Krillitanes perished, the school was swallowed up by a massive split in the ground.**
TRUE/FALSE

9. **Sarah Jane and K-9 joined the Doctor for new adventures.**
TRUE/FALSE

10. **Mickey waved off the Doctor and Rose and drove back home.**
TRUE/FALSE

RISING TO THE CHALLENGE

Ordinary people often find themselves caught up in the Doctor's action-packed existence. And *extra*-ordinary people can answer all these questions about them!

1. Whose house was taken over by monks with a sinister secret?

a) Sir Robert Muir.

b) Sir Robert MacLeish.

c) Sir Robbie McTartan.

2. What happened to him?

a) He was killed by a Dalek.

b) He was killed by a werewolf.

c) He was killed by Queen Victoria.

3. Who used his knowledge of electronics to help the Doctor defeat the Wire?

a) Mickey Smith.

b) Tommy Connolly.

c) Elton Pope.

4. **Who was the only child to escape being used by the Krillitanes?**

a) Kenny.

b) Faisal.

c) Jenny.

5. **Chloe Webber's drawings almost brought a horrifying version of someone to life. Who was it?**

a) Her gran.

b) A Cyberman.

c) Her father.

6. **Daniel Llewellyn was Project Manager of the Guinevere space probe. How did he die?**

a) He fell from a tall building.

b) He was killed by the Sycorax on board their ship.

c) He was hit by a meteorite.

7. **What name did the Doctor give the passing horse that wandered on board the SS *Madame de Pompadour*?**

a) Captain Jack.

b) Belinda.

c) Arthur.

8. **What killed Elton Pope's mother and brought Elton into contact with the Doctor for the first time?**

a) An elemental shade from the Howling Halls.

b) A Cyberman.

c) The Abzorbaloff.

PARALLEL WORLD

There's a whole world of difference between one world and its parallel counterpart. Some things seem very similar, others very different. How much do you know about the world into which the TARDIS accidentally fell?

1. **What was the name of Mickey's counterpart in the parallel world?**

a) Mickey.

b) Ricky.

c) Thickie.

2. **Pete and Jackie Tyler didn't have a daughter called Rose in this world. What did they have instead?**

a) A small dog.

b) A tiger cub.

c) A robotic mouse.

3. What was the name of John Lumic's sinister multinational company?

a) Cybus Industries.

b) Cider Industrial.

c) Metaltron Inc.

4. What electronic devices did the people of this world wear in their ears?

a) Homing beacons.

b) Ear pods.

c) Headphones.

5. Who ruled Britain on this version of Earth?

a) The prime minister.

b) The president.

c) The King.

6. Mickey's counterpart is London's Most Wanted for...?

a) Crimes against humanity.

b) Selling hot dogs without a licence.

c) Parking tickets.

7. Pete Tyler made secret broadcasts about John Lumic's activities under which codename?

a) Scorpio.

b) Pisces.

c) Gemini.

8. Who chose to remain behind on the parallel world?

a) Mickey.

b) Rose.

c) The Doctor.

FIRESIDE QUIZ TRUE OR FALSE?

When the Doctor, Mickey and Rose land on a damaged spaceship in the 51st century, they find that some windows have a very curious view... Look at the statements below and see if you can tell what's true and what's false.

1. A fireplace formed a time window linking the spaceship to 18th century France.
TRUE/FALSE

2. The Doctor saw a young girl named Reinette through the fireplace.
TRUE/FALSE

3. Reinette grew up to become the Prime Minister of France.
TRUE/FALSE

4. Clockwork repair-droids were on board the ship.
TRUE/FALSE

5. They thought they could use Reinette's brain to repair the ship's computers.
TRUE/FALSE

6. **The robots tried to use a horse to repair the other systems.**
    TRUE/FALSE

7. **The Doctor broke the link between the spaceship and France by charging through a mirror.**
    TRUE/FALSE

8. **The Doctor didn't want Reinette to join him in the TARDIS.**
    TRUE/FALSE

9. **He got to say a tender, meaningful goodbye to Reinette.**
    TRUE/FALSE

10. **The name of the spaceship was SS *Harriet Jones*.**
    TRUE/FALSE

SCORES:

8–10 Congratulations — but don't wander too near to that fireplace, or who knows where you'll end up!

5–7   The flames were a bit too dazzling, were they?

1–4   Fire is bright — but on this evidence, you're not! Better luck next time...

ANSWERS:

1. True.	2. True.	3. False.	4. True.	5. True.
6. False.	7. True.	8. False.	9. False.	10. False.

45

OLD FRIENDS

Sarah Jane was one of the Doctor's best friends, and K-9 shared many an adventure with him as well. How much do you know about this couple from the Doctor's past?

1. **What was Sarah's profession when she first met the Doctor?**
a) Dinner lady.
b) Zookeeper.
c) Journalist.

2. **What was Sarah's excuse for wanting to know all about Mr Finch's mysterious record-breaking school?**
a) She was a student teacher who wanted to work there.
b) She was writing a profile of Mr Finch for the Sunday Times.
c) She was a parent wishing to place her child there.

3. **The Doctor thought he had dropped Sarah off near her home in Croydon. But where had he *really* left her?**

a) France.

b) Cornwall.

c) Aberdeen.

4. **What does Sarah need to hear the Doctor say before she can get on with her life without him?**

a) "You were the best."

b) "I promise to save you from the Daleks."

c) "Goodbye."

5. **K-9 was originally the product of technology from the year:**

a) AD 5000.

b) AD One million.

c) AD 33.

6. **What one word does Rose use to sum up K-9's look?**

a) Retro.

b) Disco.

c) Cute.

7. Where is K-9's built-in laser stored?

a) In his nose.

b) In his tail.

c) In his eye probe.

8. What happens when K-9 is all but destroyed while defeating the Krillitanes?

a) Rose throws him on the scrap heap.

b) Sarah keeps his tail as a souvenir.

c) The Doctor rebuilds him from scratch.

ALIEN IDENTIFICATION

Look at the fragments on the following pages of some of the aliens the Doctor has encountered. How many do you recognise?

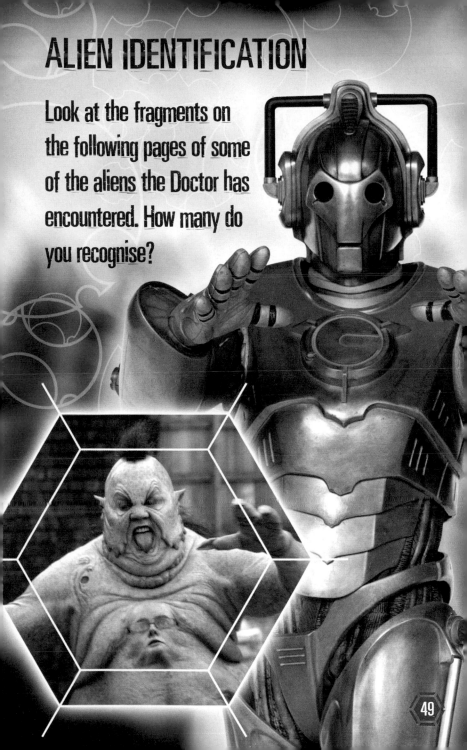

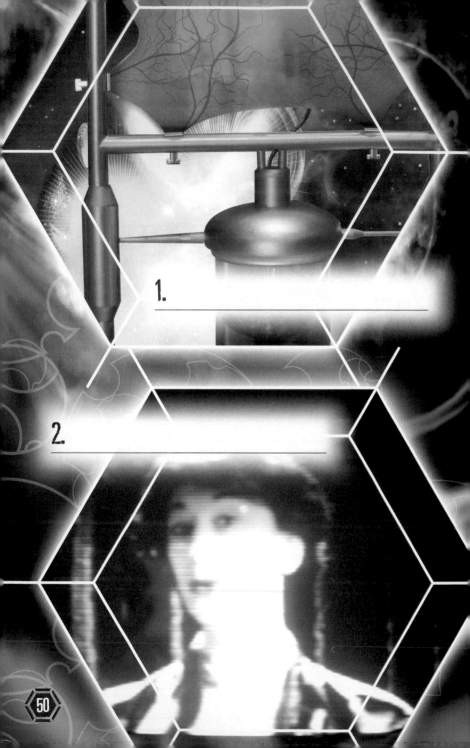

1. _____

2. _____

3.
_____

4.
_____

5.

6.

7.

8.

9.

10.

11.

12.

99

ANSWERS:

1. Cassandra

2. The Wire

3. The Face of Boe

4. Dalek

5. Clockwork droid

6. Slitheen

7. Werewolf

8. Sycorax

9. The Beast

10 Emperor Dalek

11. K-9

12. Ood

HOW EVIL ARE YOU?

Now it's time to get in touch with your inner monster! Forget bravery, self-sacrifice and passion. Just how dark and deadly could you be? Try to think like an alien — would you be as hard as a Cyberman or as mild as an unpossessed Ood? Take the test below and find out...

1. **You find an alien planet that is largely uninhabited and strategically sound. Do you:**

a) Set up a base so you can use the planet as a means of invading nearby worlds.

b) Hunt about for intelligent life and try to offer yourself into slavery.

c) Seek out all life forms, eradicate them, amass an army and CONQUER THE GALAXY!

2. **While travelling through deep space you pick up a distress call from a damaged spaceship. Do you:**

a) Board the ship and upgrade all personnel in your image?

b) Seek out the loneliest crew members and try to make them feel happier.

c) Slaughter everyone on board.

3. **Shortly after landing on a planet, you discover a puppy farm filled with cute little beagles. Do you:**

a) Ignore them. These creatures pose no threat, nor can they aid you.

b) Empathise with their longing for love and freedom.

c) Absorb their brain energy, what little there is, and destroy them.

4. Alone in a vast city, you need power to repair your spaceship. How would you prefer to get it?

a) Siphon it from a nearby city slowly, so as not to alert others to your presence.

b) Offer yourself into slavery for several years in exchange for the energy.

c) Exterminate all life in the city and divert all power supplies to your ship.

5. Caught up in the fringes of a warp-ellipse, you find yourself propelled fifty years into the past, out of contact with your fleet. Do you:

a) Lie dormant for fifty years, then continue with your existence as normal.

b) Sustain yourself through the long, lean years by sharing your loneliness with suitable life forms.

c) Obliterate life on the nearest planet, then broadcast to others of your kind that your plans for galactic domination can be brought forward.

6. **You encounter a life form who takes one look at you and starts pleading for his life in terror. Do you:**

a) Upgrade him or delete him if he is not compatible.

b) Empathise with his pain and try to ease it.

c) Blast the weakling scum out of existence.

7. **As you travel through intergalactic space you witness the beautiful, ultra-rare, awe-inspiring spectacle of millions of comets orbiting a quasar. Do you:**

a) Ignore it. Pretty views are irrelevant.

b) Dart in and out among the asteroids, using them as an enormous playground.

c) Vaporise the comets one by one. Some day they could shelter life forms that could threaten your kind.

8. You encounter the Doctor. Do you:

a) Delete him at once. Rogue elements are incompatible and must be removed.

b) Scream.

c) Blow him up. Then blow up everyone who ever knew him.

HOW DID YOU DO?

Mostly As:

You're a cold, emotionless sort of monster, with more than a hint of Cyberman about you. You are governed by harsh, unimaginative logic. Lacking emotions and not understanding the concepts of boredom and wasted time, you are prepared to wait as long as it is necessary to get your sinister tasks done. That sort of dedication to the cause is truly frightening, as is your total lack of imagination or wonder. You probably haven't even got the sense to beware the Doctor! With his compassion, conscience and quirky intellect he will run rings round you every time!

Mostly Bs:

You are proof that not all aliens are evil and nasty, at least not all the time! Like the Isolus, some of them just want understanding, or love or company, or in the Ood's case, even just to be told what to do so that they have a purpose in life. If you encounter the Doctor and you are in trouble, do not fight against him or doubt his powers. He can turn a seemingly hopeless situation into a fighting chance of triumph.

Mostly Cs:

Hmm. You're not exactly cuddly and fluffy, are you? In fact, you're downright horrible. A spiteful, calculating, intolerant, vicious killer with a pathological hatred for anything that's different from your own kind, you don't have a pleasant atom in your biomass. In fact, you make most Daleks seem like laid-back fun-seekers. Congratulations! You make a truly *monstrous* monster!

62

TV TERROR TRUE OR FALSE?

You've probably been told that watching TV can give you square eyes. But in 1953, the Doctor and Rose found that watching telly could do far worse things to your face! Say true or false to these statements about *The Idiot's Lantern*...

1. **The Doctor and Rose came to Earth wanting to see the Beatles.**
   TRUE/FALSE

2. **They thought they had landed in New York.**
   TRUE/FALSE

3. **A disembodied creature called the Cord was controlling TV signals.**
   TRUE/FALSE

4. **The creature took the form of a prim and proper TV presenter.**
   TRUE/FALSE

5. **The creature absorbed electrical energy from people's brains.**
   TRUE/FALSE

6. It also sucked their legs into its television sets.
   TRUE/FALSE

7. A backstreet TV salesman called Mr Magoo was helping the Cord.
   TRUE/FALSE

8. Rose's face was sucked off by the creature.
   TRUE/FALSE

9. Everyone was watching the Queen's Silver Jubilee on TV when the creature struck.
   TRUE/FALSE

10. The Doctor was able to trap the creature inside a videotape.
    TRUE/FALSE

BLASTS FROM THE PAST

The TARDIS often pitches up in the past, where the Doctor and Rose become caught up in sinister events not noted in any history book... How much do you remember of their past journeys?

1. **In what year did the Doctor and Rose meet Queen Victoria?**

a) 1479.

b) 1879.

c) 1979.

2. **A werewolf entity fell to Earth in 1540, near to a monastery — but where?**

a) The Glen of St Catherine, Scotland.

b) The Place de la Concorde, France.

c) The Highlands of Newport, Wales.

3. **What was the real name of Madame de Pompadour?**

a) Emily Fish.   b) Jeanne-Antoinette Poisson.

c) Nigella Stoat.

4. How old was the girl who would become Madame de Pompadour when the Doctor first met her?

a) Seven.

b) Sixteen.

c) Two.

5. The clockwork robots wanted to take Madame de Pompadour's head to fix their ship's computers, but why did they have to wait till she was 37 years old?

a) Because they needed the brain of an experienced woman.

b) Because the ship was 37 years old and the head had to be compatible.

c) Because their lucky number was 37.

6. What historical event in 1953 did the Wire choose for its Time of Manifestation?

a) The coronation of Queen Elizabeth II.

b) The climbing of Mount Everest.

c) The end of sweets rationing.

7. In 1953, who did the security guard at the Alexandra Palace TV transmitter believe the Doctor to be?

a) A Dalek.

b) The King of Belgium.

c) A choc ice vendor.

8. One dark night in the 1970s, the Doctor vanquished a living shadow in a house in Bexley Heath, which was home to which little boy?

a) Mickey Smith.

b) Tommy Connolly.

c) Elton Pope.

THE SATAN PIT TRUE OR FALSE?

Remember the terrifying time the Doctor and Rose had on an impossible planet? Luckily answering this quiz is *perfectly* possible, if you can just say whether the following statements are true or false...

1. The TARDIS landed on a base on a planet orbiting a black hole.
    TRUE/FALSE

2. The planet's name was Krop Tor.
    TRUE/FALSE

3. The crew of the base there were served by a race called the Ood.
    TRUE/FALSE

4. The planet was protected from the Black Hole by an incredible power source sitting on its surface.
    TRUE/FALSE

5. An ancient force known as the Beast lived in a luxury hotel deep within the planet.
    TRUE/FALSE

6. **The Doctor climbed down a long ladder into the Pit to confront the Beast.**
TRUE/FALSE

7. **The body of the Beast was imprisoned but its mind was in one of the crew.**
TRUE/FALSE

8. **Rose defeated the crew member by shooting him.**
TRUE/FALSE

9. **The Doctor used the TARDIS to rescue Rose and the surviving crew.**
TRUE/FALSE

10. **All the Ood survived the destruction of the base on Krop Tor.**
TRUE/FALSE

THE DREADED DALEKS

Just as the Doctor thinks he's got enough on his hands with a Cyberman invasion of Earth, he finds the Daleks are also on the scene. But these are no ordinary Daleks... How much do you remember about them?

1. **How did the Daleks guarding the Genesis Ark escape the carnage of the Time War?**

a) In an unmarked rocket ship.

b) In a Void Ship.

c) In an Isolus cocoon.

2. **These four Daleks belonged to a special, secret order above and beyond the Emperor himself. What was it called?**

a) The Cult of Skaro.

b) The League of Dalek Conquerors.

c) The Future Dalek Pantheon.

3. What set these Daleks apart from all others?

a) They had two gun sticks.

b) They spoke in soft Yorkshire accents.

c) They had individual names.

4. What is the skin of a Dalek made from?

a) Polycarbide.

b) Bronze.

c) Exterminatum.

5. How do Daleks extract brainwaves?

a) With their gunsticks.

b) With the sensor globes on their skirt sections.

c) With their sucker sticks.

6. Who designed and built the Genesis Ark?

a) The Daleks.

b) The Time Lords.

c) The Cybermen.

7. What was its purpose?

a) To be a prison ship holding millions of Daleks.

b) To be a handy transport for Dalek invaders.

c) To be a means of escaping floods on alien worlds.

8. What happened to the Daleks when the Doctor opened the Void and reversed it?

a) They were sucked into the dead space between parallel worlds.

b) They exploded.

c) They self-destructed.

0–3 EXTERMINATE!
out your brainwaves!
4–6 A fair score, but Daleks won't fight each other for the chance to suck
7–8 You are a Dalek expert!

SCORES:

5. c	6. b	7. a	8. a
1. b	2. a	3. c	4. a

ANSWERS:

LOVE AND MONSTERS
TRUE OR FALSE?

The Doctor has touched all our lives... but some have got his fingerprints all over them! If you recall the strange story of Elton Pope, you should be able to sort the statements below into true and false!

1. **Elton was born in 1945.**
    TRUE/FALSE

2. **Elton was out shopping when the Nestene Consciousness brought its dummies to life.**
    TRUE/FALSE

3. **Elton did not see the Slitheen ship crash into Big Ben.**
    TRUE/FALSE

4. **The Doctor was the focus of a group of believers who called their organisation JILL.**
    TRUE/FALSE

5. **A man called Victor Kennedy visited the group, hunting for the Doctor.**
    TRUE/FALSE

6. **Elton met Jackie Tyler in an Italian restaurant.**
   TRUE/FALSE

7. **Jackie found out he was using her to find out about Rose.**
   TRUE/FALSE

8. **Victor Kennedy turned out to be a monster called the Abzorbaloff.**
   TRUE/FALSE

9. **The Abzorbaloff came from the Daleks' twin planet.**
   TRUE/FALSE

10. **The Abzorbaloff was finally defeated when he was absorbed by the Earth.**
    TRUE/FALSE

watch it again!

SCORES:

8–10 Hope you made a video diary of your breathtaking quiz success!

5–7 Not bad — but you could do with reviewing your footage more often!

0–4 You didn't absorb much of this story at all, did you? Go back and watch it again!

ANSWERS:

1. False.   2. True.   3. False.   4. False.   5. True.

6. False.   7. True.   8. True.   9. False.   10. True.

IDENTITY PARADE

The Doctor has incredible recall, and can identify aliens from only the slimmest of clues. How would you fare? Match each description to the creatures listed below!

1. A meek slave race who live for orders.
2. Machine-creatures who were once human, emotions removed and replaced with steel.
3. Empathic beings of intense emotion.
4. Creatures of pure hate inside near-indestructible travel machines.
5. A hideous monster that thrives on absorbing others.
6. An evil intelligence that feeds on brain activity.

a) Daleks   b) Ood   c) Abzorbaloff

d) Cybermen   e) Isolus   f) The Wire

ANSWERS:

1.b	2.d	3.e
4.a	5.c	6.f

SCORES:

5–6   With knowledge like this, you could write the Big Book of Mind-Boggling Creatures!

3–4   With knowledge like this, you could maybe contribute a few pages to the Big Book of Mind-Boggling Creatures!

0–2   With knowledge like this you should probably *read* the Big Book of Mind-Boggling Creatures. It's published in 2145, available in all good Thragstores... don't get trampled in the rush!

QUESTIONS FOR ANSWERS

The following random quiz questions passed through an ion storm and came out in a jumble. In each case you'll find the correct answer has been given to you first — so now you must choose the *question* that would get you that answer! Good luck...

I. "EXTERMINATE!"

a)   What is the battle cry of a Cyberman?

b)   What is the war cry of a Dalek?

c)   What is the service squeak of an Ood?

2. A satsuma.

a)   What was the first thing the Doctor asked for after regenerating?

b)   What fruit did the Doctor use to finally defeat the Sycorax leader?

c)   What fruit did the Doctor use to make cocktails in 18ᵗʰ century France?

3. By passing through a time window disguised as a revolving fireplace.

a)   How did the Doctor first meet Reinette in 18ᵗʰ century France?

b)   How did the Doctor cheat in a race against Rose?

c)   How did Mickey and Rose get hold of some space-age fire extinguishers?

4. Five.

a) How many repair droids are on board
SS *Madame de Pompadour*?

b) How many Cat Sisters are working on New Earth?

c) A Cyberman's hand has how many digits?

5. Clom.

a) What is the twin planet of Raxacoricofallapatorius?

b) What is the name of Skaro's moon?

c) What is the opposite of festiniogg?

**6. It used the power of the Olympic flame
to travel back into space.**

a) How did the Wire escape execution?

b) How did the stray Isolus pod eventually leave Earth?

c) How did the Face of Boe leave the hospital on New Earth?

0–2   Hmm. Maybe you don't actually *have* a mind!

when you took the test.

3–4   Oh well, maybe some random ion flux was messing with your mind

Well done!

5–6   You are not easily fazed or deterred from picking the right option.

SCORES:

1. b   2. b   3. a   4. c   5. a   6. b

ANSWERS (OR RATHER QUESTIONS):

ODD ONE OUT

In each of the groupings below there is an odd one out... Seek it out and exterminate it!

1. Thay, Lumic, Jast, Caan.

2. Parallel Jackie Tyler, Yvonne Hartman, Pete Tyler, Sally Phelan.

3. Elvis, Ian Dury and the Blockheads, Robbie Williams, Spice Girls.

4. Elton Pope, Ursula Blake, Rita Connolly, Mr Skinner.

5. Rose, Sarah Jane, Mickey, The Doctor undercover as a teacher.

6. A horse, an eyeball, a time window, a barrel of Krillitanes oil.

ANSWERS:

1. Lumic — the others are all the names of Daleks.

2. Pete Tyler — the others were all converted into Cybermen.

3. Robbie Williams — the TARDIS went off course while the Doctor was trying to take Rose to see the others in concert.

4. Rita Connolly — the others all belonged to the LINDA organisation.

5. Rose — the others all share the surname Smith.

6. The Krillitanes oil — the others could all be found on the SS *Madame de Pompadour*.

SCORES

5–6 A fantastic score in a very hard quiz. You must know more about the Doctor than Victor Kennedy!

3–4 Still a pretty impressive result. Why not start a secret society to study the Doctor more closely?

0–2 Oops. Looks like the Abzorbaloff has already been your way and sucked out your brain cells! Better luck next time!

FEAR HER TRUE OR FALSE?

When the TARDIS landed in East London in 2012, things were far from being *picture*-perfect... Can you say whether the statements below are true or false?

1. The Doctor wanted to take Rose to the London Olympics.
   TRUE/FALSE

2. He and Rose learned that several children had disappeared from the same street.
   TRUE/FALSE

3. To investigate, the Doctor posed as a private detective hired by the Olympic committee.
   TRUE/FALSE

4. He found that living things were being snatched out of space-time using ionic power.
   TRUE/FALSE

5. Rose was almost eaten by an intelligent garage door.
   TRUE/FALSE

6. **They learned that anyone drawn by a girl called Chloe became trapped inside her living pictures.**
   TRUE/FALSE

7. **Chloe was being controlled by the Cybermen.**
   TRUE/FALSE

8. **An Isolus pod had crashed nearby, and the Isolus was very, very lonely.**
   TRUE/FALSE

9. **It wanted to take over the universe.**
   TRUE/FALSE

10. **The Doctor could not free Chloe and the Isolus with the help of the Olympic torch.**
    TRUE/FALSE

THE TORCHWOOD FACTOR

The Doctor hears rumours and whispers of Torchwood long before he encounters them for himself. When he does, things will never be the same again... And they may not be for you if you don't do well in this quiz!

1. Who founded the Torchwood Institute?

a)   Queen Elizabeth II.

b)   King Louis XV.

c)   Queen Victoria.

2. Why was Torchwood founded?

a)   To blow up alien planets.

b)   To provide cheap space travel to other galaxies.

c)   To keep Britain great and defended against the alien hordes.

3. **Who was named as an enemy of the crown in the Torchwood Foundation Charter of 1879?**

a) The Daleks.

b) The Doctor.

c) Mickey Smith.

4. **What is the Torchwood Institute's Motto?**

a) Kill all aliens.

b) Love thy alien.

c) If it's alien, it's ours.

5. **What type of craft was shot down by Torchwood just off the Shetland Isles, ten years ago?**

a) A Dalek battleship.

b) A Jathaa Sun Glider.

c) An Isolus hover-scooter.

6. **Why was the Torchwood Tower built in a particular part of London?**

a) To gain access to a hole in the fabric of reality.

b) It was a cheap place to build.

c) To mark Queen Victoria's birthplace.

7. What lethal weapon took Torchwood scientists eight years to get working?

a) The particle gun.

b) The glitter gun.

c) The radium vapour ray.

8. Where did Torchwood find a supply of magna-clamps, enabling them to lift heavy objects with ease?

a) Under a bush in Utah.

b) In a spaceship buried at the base of Mount Snowdon.

c) In an alien lab orbiting Saturn.

9. Who did Captain Zachary Flane of Sanctuary Base Six represent?

a) The Torchwood Archive.

b) The Torchwood Galaxy.

c) The Torchwood Retirement Home.

10. What creatures were contained within the Sphere in Torchwood Tower?

a) Cybermen.

b) Daleks.

c) The Ood.

11. What was responsible for corrupting all Torchwood's data-files on Rose Tyler?

a   A magna-worm complex.

b) A Bad Wolf virus.

c) A hard drive super-crash.

12. What happened to the Torchwood Institute on the Parallel World?

a) The People's Republic took control of it.

b) It was destroyed by Daleks.

c) It was disbanded by the British President.

QUALITY QUOTES

Who *first* said the following memorable words?
Clear out your ears and see if any of these
quality quotes stick in your mind...

1. **"Oh, you never want to listen to reason."**

a) Rose.

b) The Doctor.

c) A Cyberman.

2. **"Sycorax strong!**
   Sycorax mighty!
   Sycorax ROCK!"

a) Harriet Jones.

b) The Sycorax.

c) The Face of Boe.

3. "I'm COMMMMMIIIIIIIIIIIIINNNGGGGGGG..."

a) Father Angelo.

b) The picture of Chloe Webber's dad in the back of the wardrobe.

c) The Abzorbaloff.

4. "Oh my God – I'm a chav!"

a) Cassandra.

b) Queen Victoria.

c) The Beast.

5. "Pain and loss and grief, they define us as much as happiness or love. If it's a world, or a relationship, everything has its time. And everything ends."

a) A Cyberman.

b) Mickey.

c) Sarah.

6. "We are Human Point Two. Every citizen will receive a free upgrade. You will become like us."

a) A Cyberman.

b) The Duke of Manhattan.

c) An Ood.

7. "This is your freedom! Free to die! You're going into the black hole, and I'm riding with you!"

a) The Ood.

b) The Doctor.

c) The Face of Boe.

8. "Affirmative!"

a) The Wire.

b) The Daleks.

c) K-9.

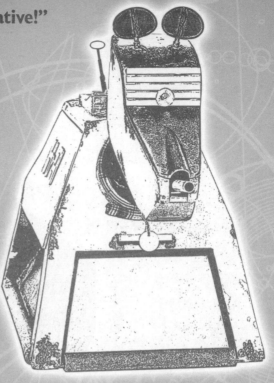

DOOMSDAY! TRUE OR FALSE?

When worlds collide and the Doctor's two deadliest enemies show up, you know you're in for a brilliant adventure — and that life will never be the same again for anyone... Say if the statements below are true or false — if you dare!

1. The Doctor and Rose arrived on Earth to find mysterious ghosts were appearing all over the world.
TRUE/FALSE

2. The Doctor tried to communicate with a ghost and it was very helpful and cooperative. TRUE/FALSE

3. The Doctor was captured by Torchwood.
TRUE/FALSE

4. He was shown a mysterious Void Ship that looked like an enormous cube.
TRUE/FALSE

5. The Void Ship had punched through reality, allowing the ghosts to slip through from a parallel world. TRUE/FALSE

6. **The ghosts were really the Ood in disguise.** TRUE/FALSE

7. **There were Daleks inside the Sphere, along with something called the Genesis Ark.** TRUE/FALSE

8. **The Daleks teamed up with the Cybermen to invade Earth.**
TRUE/FALSE

9. **Millions of Ood were set free from within the Genesis Ark.**
TRUE/FALSE

10. **The Doctor defeated the invaders by sending them to a dimensional hot spot on the Moon.**
TRUE/FALSE

like this? Watch the proper adventure again as soon as possible!

0–4 What mad version of events did *you* sit through to come up with a score in your head?

5–7 Your memory seems a bit hazy — maybe there's a bit of Voidstuff stuck

adventures — well done!

8–10 You stayed faithful to the Doctor right to the explosive climax of his

SCORES

6. False.	7. True.	8. False.	9. False.	10. False.
1. True.	2. False.	3. True.	4. False.	5. True.

ANSWERS:

THE MEGA CHALLENGE

This final quiz is designed to test the outermost reaches of your *Doctor Who* knowledge. It's longer, harder and more challenging than the others… so if you have any Krillitanes oil to hand, you'd better fry up some chips and scoff them down before you read another line! If you want to make it even tougher, set yourself a three-minute time limit for all 30 questions!

Good luck. Ready for the quiz ride of a lifetime? Then… get set and GO!

1. **How many different versions of New York have there been by the year five billion?**

a   Twenty.

b)   Fifteen.

c)   Forty-three.

2. **What effect does seeing the Sphere have on onlookers?**

a)   It makes you want to stroke it.

b)   It makes you want to run and hide.

c)   It gives you the runs.

3. **In what form does Ursula Blake live on?**

a)   A bucket of mud.

b)   A parka.

c)   A paving stone.

4. **How long do the Isolus children take to grow up?**

a)   Five seconds.

b)   One year.

c)   Thousands and thousands of years.

5. In which galaxy can New Earth be found?

a) M87.

b) M1.

c) Andromeda.

6. Who accidentally reactivated the Genesis Ark?

a) Rose.

b) The Doctor.

c) Mickey.

7. Rose gives Jackie the gift of Bazoolium. What can it be used for?

a) To make all clocks in a house tell the exact time.

b) To tell the weather.

c) To play the Bazoo.

8. **What was the name of the diamond in Queen Victoria's possession, used to defeat the werewolf creature?**

a) The Gem of Plenty.

b) The Taj Glass-stone.

c) The Koh-i-noor.

9. **What does LINDA stand for?**

a) Local Individually Noticed Doctor Activity.

b) London Investigation 'N' Detective Agency.

c) Legal Inquest Naming Doctor's Associates.

10. **What type of creature was Cassandra's devoted acolyte, Chip?**

a) A force-grown clone.

b) A New Human.

c) A Slitheen.

11. **The spaceship SS *Madame de Pompadour* hailed from which century?**

a) The 10th.

b) The 22nd.

c) The 51st.

12. Which of the following coronations was not referred to by the Doctor when he visited 1953?

a) The Fragrant Arrows of the Half-Light, numbers eight through fifteen.

b) William the Silent's.

c) King Zahoo of Michigan's.

13. To function, the Genesis Ark needs an area of what size?

a) Thirty square miles.

b) Twenty round units.

c) Fifteen rectangular kilometres.

14. Who were seeking to unravel the so-called Skasas Paradigm in order to control all of creation?

a) The Daleks.

b) The Krillitanes.

c) The Reapers.

15. Who was present at the Fall of Arcadia during the Time War?

a) Mickey.

b) The Cyber Controller.

c) The Doctor.

16. Why do the Ood crave orders?

a) They are paid per command they are given.

b) They have nothing else in their lives.

c) They are sent to slave school from birth.

17. What was required to reactivate the Genesis Ark?

a) Electricity.

b) A plasma bombardment.

c) The touch of a time traveller.

18. How many brothers and sisters does an Isolus have?

a) Four billion.

b) Four hundred.

c) Four.

19. What was the last occasion on which Cassandra was told she was beautiful?

a) A shopping expedition to Harrodos Major.

b) An art gallery opening hosted by the Magna-being of Thorr.

c) A drinks party for the Ambassador of Thrace.

20. To the Abzorbaloff, what did Ursula Blake taste like?

a) Chicken.

b) Peaches.

c) A slime-slott from the planet Graar.

21. What is supposed to happen to someone generating a telepathic field measuring Basic 100?

a) They collapse.

b) They can read minds.

c) Instant brain death.

22. What blood type were the humans affected by Sycorax blood control?

a) Any type.

b) A positive.

c) D minus.

23. What is the chief visual difference between a Cyberman and a Cyber Controller?

a) Its brain is visible through its helmet.

b) It is much taller.

c) It has an extra set of arms.

24. Which planet do the evil alien Graske come from?

a) Griffoth.

b) Scarith.

c) Earth.

25. What was the full name of the base on Krop Tor?

a) Sanctuary Base One.

b) Sanctuary Base Six.

c) Torchwood Retreat.

26. What did the Doctor's special cardboard glasses enable him to see?

a) Invisible Daleks.

b) Voidstuff.

c) Hidden werewolves.

27. Who summoned the Doctor to New Earth?

a)   Cal MacNannovitch.

b)   The Duke of Manhattan.

c)   The Face of Boe.

28. Where did the organisation LINDA gather to discuss the Doctor?

a)   A village hall in Loopers Lane.

b)   Underneath the old lock-up on Maccateer Street.

c)   In a church vestry on Venus Avenue.

29. What was the name of Cassandra's faithful servant?

a)   Fish.

b)   Chip.

c)   Peez.

30. What was the official name of the Black Hole that helps imprison the Beast?

a)   K37 Gem 5.

b)   Roger-K-Roger.

c)   Holeus Blackus.

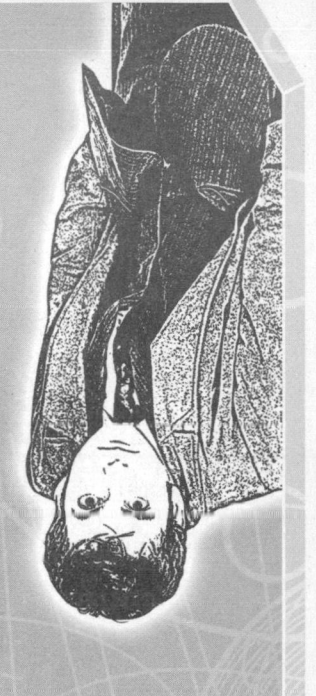

ANSWERS:

1. b	2. b	3. c	4. c
5. a	6. c	7. b	8. c
9. b	10. a	11. c	12. c
13. a	14. b	15. c	16. b
17. c	18. a	19. c	20. a
21. c	22. b	23. a	24. a
25. b	26. b	27. c	28. b
29. b	30. a		

SCORES:

26–30 An astounding display of *Doctor Who* knowledge!
Who needs Krillitanes oil? You're a natural time travel genius.

22–25 A result to be proud of — if the fate of the world depended on your
in-depth *Doctor Who* knowledge, you'd stand a good chance of
saving it!

17–21 A solid foundation upon which to build your knowledge of the
Doctor and his universe.

10–16 Cheer up, you're still smarter than a malfunctioning repair droid!

5–9 OK, so you're *not* smarter than a malfunctioning repair droid!

0–4 Has the Wire been busy sucking out your brain impulses again?
Get better soon!